MAD LIBS

ROCK 'N' ROLL
MAD LIBS

By Roger Price and Leonard Stern

PSS!

PRICE STERN SLOAN

An Imprint of Penguin Group (USA) Inc.

PRICE STERN SLOAN
Published by the Penguin Group
Penguin Group (USA) Inc., 375 Hudson Street, New York, New York 10014, USA
Penguin Group (Canada), 90 Eglinton Avenue East, Suite 700,
Toronto, Ontario M4P 2Y3, Canada
(a division of Pearson Penguin Canada Inc.)
Penguin Books Ltd., 80 Strand, London WC2R 0RL, England
Penguin Group Ireland, 25 St. Stephen's Green, Dublin 2, Ireland
(a division of Penguin Books Ltd.)
Penguin Group (Australia), 250 Camberwell Road, Camberwell, Victoria 3124, Australia
(a division of Pearson Australia Group Pty. Ltd.)
Penguin Books India Pvt. Ltd., 11 Community Centre,
Panchsheel Park, New Delhi—110 017, India
Penguin Group (NZ), 67 Apollo Drive, Rosedale, North Shore 0632, New Zealand
(a division of Pearson New Zealand Ltd.)
Penguin Books (South Africa) (Pty.) Ltd., 24 Sturdee Avenue,
Rosebank, Johannesburg 2196, South Africa

Penguin Books Ltd., Registered Offices:
80 Strand, London WC2R 0RL, England

ISBN 978-0-8431-2695-2

7 9 10 8 6

MAD LIBS® is a game for people who don't like games!
It can be played by one, two, three, four, or forty.

● RIDICULOUSLY SIMPLE DIRECTIONS

In this tablet you will find stories containing blank spaces where words
are left out. One player, the READER, selects one of these stories. The
READER does not tell anyone what the story is about. Instead, he/she asks
the other players, the WRITERS, to give him/her words. These words are
used to fill in the blank spaces in the story.

● TO PLAY

The READER asks each WRITER in turn to call out a word—an adjective or
a noun or whatever the space calls for—and uses them to fill in the blank
spaces in the story. The result is a MAD LIBS® game.

When the READER then reads the completed MAD LIBS® game to the other
players, they will discover that they have written a story that is fantastic,
screamingly funny, shocking, silly, crazy, or just plain dumb—depending
upon which words each WRITER called out.

● EXAMPLE (*Before* and *After*)

" _____ !" he said _____
      EXCLAMATION   ADVERB

as he jumped into his convertible _____ and
                                 NOUN

drove off with his _____ wife.
                 ADJECTIVE

" *Ouch* !" he said *stupidly*
      EXCLAMATION   ADVERB

as he jumped into his convertible *cat* and
                                 NOUN

drove off with his *brave* wife.
                 ADJECTIVE

In case you have forgotten what adjectives, adverbs, nouns, and verbs are, here is a quick review:

An ADJECTIVE describes something or somebody. *Lumpy*, *soft*, *ugly*, *messy*, and *short* are adjectives.

An ADVERB tells how something is done. It modifies a verb and usually ends in "ly." *Modestly*, *stupidly*, *greedily*, and *carefully* are adverbs.

A NOUN is the name of a person, place, or thing. *Sidewalk*, *umbrella*, *bridle*, *bathtub*, and *nose* are nouns.

A VERB is an action word. *Run*, *pitch*, *jump*, and *swim* are verbs. Put the verbs in past tense if the directions say PAST TENSE. *Ran*, *pitched*, *jumped*, and *swam* are verbs in the past tense.

When we ask for A PLACE, we mean any sort of place: a country or city (*Spain*, *Cleveland*) or a room (*bathroom*, *kitchen*).

An EXCLAMATION or SILLY WORD is any sort of funny sound, gasp, grunt, or outcry, like *Wow!*, *Ouch!*, *Whomp!*, *Ick!*, and *Gadzooks!*

When we ask for specific words, like a NUMBER, a COLOR, an ANIMAL, or a PART OF THE BODY, we mean a word that is one of those things, like *seven*, *blue*, *horse*, or *head*.

When we ask for a PLURAL, it means more than one. For example, *cat* pluralized is *cats*.

MAD LIBS® is fun to play with friends, but you can also play it by yourself! To begin with, DO NOT look at the story on the page below. Fill in the blanks on this page with the words called for. Then, using the words you have selected, fill in the blank spaces in the story.

Now you've created your own hilarious MAD LIBS® game!

FAMILY ROCK BAND

ADJECTIVE _____

LAST NAME _____

ADJECTIVE _____

NOUN _____

ADJECTIVE _____

PLURAL NOUN _____

NOUN _____

ADJECTIVE _____

PLURAL NOUN _____

NOUN _____

ADJECTIVE _____

PLURAL NOUN _____

ADJECTIVE _____

ADJECTIVE _____

NOUN _____

ADVERB _____

LETTER OF THE ALPHABET _____

NOUN _____

MAD LIBS®

FAMILY ROCK BAND

I don't come from your average ___Smelly___ family. That's
                                    ADJECTIVE

because we're all part of the ___Jones___ Family rock band
                                LAST NAME

and we lead a very ___snarky___ life. For example, by not
                        ADJECTIVE

shaving his ___cheese___ every morning, my dad saves enough
                NOUN

time to practice the ___soft___ drums. My brother doesn't
                        ADJECTIVE

participate in extracurricular ___Trees___ at school because
                                PLURAL NOUN

he plays the electric ___underwear___. My ___shiny___ sister doesn't
                        NOUN   ADJECTIVE

have time to date ___beads___ because she sings lead vocals and
                    PLURAL NOUN

practices for four or five hours every ___Game___. When I'm not
                                        NOUN

writing our ___Tough___ songs, I'm tickling the ___lipsticks___
                ADJECTIVE   PLURAL NOUN

on the keyboard, so I don't have any free time either. Finally, Mom is

our ___Furry___ manager. She books our band to play at
        ADJECTIVE

weddings, ___wet___ sixteens, and ___football___
            ADJECTIVE   NOUN

mitzvahs. Maybe someday, if we practice ___slowly___ enough,
                                            ADVERB

we'll get to make a music video for ___B___-TV and play
                                LETTER OF THE ALPHABET

sold-out shows at Madison Square ___TV___!
                                    NOUN

MAD LIBS® is fun to play with friends, but you can also play it by yourself! To begin with, DO NOT look at the story on the page below. Fill in the blanks on this page with the words called for. Then, using the words you have selected, fill in the blank spaces in the story.

Now you've created your own hilarious MAD LIBS® game!

TEST YOUR MUSICAL IQ

NOUN _____

ADJECTIVE _____

ADJECTIVE _____

OCCUPATION _____

ADJECTIVE _____

PERSON IN ROOM _____

ADJECTIVE _____

ADJECTIVE _____

VERB _____

NOUN _____

VERB _____

SILLY WORD _____

NOUN _____

ADVERB _____

NOUN _____

NOUN _____

MAD LIBS®

TEST YOUR MUSICAL IQ

Think you're a true music __egg__ ? Test your knowledge in
                        NOUN

the __curly__ quiz below!
      ADJECTIVE

1. Which __shiney__ singer and part-time __lawyer__ recently
          ADJECTIVE   OCCUPATION

   won the Grammy for " __Sparkly__ Album of the Year"?
                         ADJECTIVE

   Answer: __ike__
            PERSON IN ROOM

2. What is the __sharp__ definition of the musical term *allegro*?
                ADJECTIVE

   Answer: __round__
            ADJECTIVE

3. What was the first rock 'n' __run__ song to hit number
                                VERB

   one on the __bagle__ charts?
               NOUN

   Answer: " __play__ Around the Clock"
            VERB

4. What was Wolfgang __zonk__ Mozart's last opera?
                      SILLY WORD

   Answer: *The Magic* __dog__
                        NOUN

5. Which song is always sung __slowly__ prior to American
                              ADVERB

   sporting events like __plate__ -ball games?
                        NOUN

   Answer: "The Star-Spangled __Baseball__"
                               NOUN

MAD LIBS® is fun to play with friends, but you can also play it by yourself! To begin with, DO NOT look at the story on the page below. Fill in the blanks on this page with the words called for. Then, using the words you have selected, fill in the blank spaces in the story.

Now you've created your own hilarious MAD LIBS® game!

INTERVIEW WITH A ROCK STAR

ADJECTIVE _____

PLURAL NOUN _____

NOUN _____

ADJECTIVE _____

ADJECTIVE _____

A PLACE _____

ADJECTIVE _____

NOUN _____

NOUN _____

NOUN _____

PLURAL NOUN _____

PLURAL NOUN _____

ADJECTIVE _____

PLURAL NOUN _____

NOUN _____

MAD LIBS®
INTERVIEW WITH A ROCK STAR

The famous Johnny Rockstar, from the ___creamy___ band
                                      ADJECTIVE

The ___tatertots___, recently gave an exclusive interview to the
      PLURAL NOUN

___hair___ City Times. Here's how it went:
  NOUN

Interviewer: When did you get your first ___Shy___ break?
                                            ADJECTIVE

Rockstar: The band had just finished playing at a/an ___curvy___
                                                        ADJECTIVE

lounge in (the) _____ when a/an _____ music
                A PLACE   ADJECTIVE

executive walked up to me and said, "Hey, kid. You've got

real _____ quality!" She signed the band to a three-
          NOUN

_____ deal with her record company! We couldn't believe
    NOUN

our _____!
        NOUN

Interviewer: What advice would you give to aspiring young

_____?
PLURAL NOUN

Rockstar: Don't ever let go of your _____.
                                      PLURAL NOUN

Interviewer: What's the best part of your _____ rock star life?
                                             ADJECTIVE

Rockstar: Getting mail from my loyal and devoted _____.
                                                    PLURAL NOUN

Oh, and seeing my _____ in the newspaper!
                      NOUN

MAD LIBS® is fun to play with friends, but you can also play it by yourself! To begin with, DO NOT look at the story on the page below. Fill in the blanks on this page with the words called for. Then, using the words you have selected, fill in the blank spaces in the story.

Now you've created your own hilarious MAD LIBS® game!

MY FIRST ROCK CONCERT

VERB ENDING IN "ING" _____

PLURAL NOUN _____

PART OF THE BODY _____

ADVERB _____

ADVERB _____

PLURAL NOUN _____

ADJECTIVE _____

PART OF THE BODY (PLURAL) _____

ADVERB _____

ADJECTIVE _____

ADJECTIVE _____

ADJECTIVE _____

SAME ADJECTIVE _____

NOUN _____

ADJECTIVE _____

NOUN _____

PART OF THE BODY _____

MAD LIBS®

MY FIRST ROCK CONCERT

The first band I ever saw in concert was the _____
                                                VERB ENDING IN "ING"

_____. Before the show began, I stood shoulder-to-
PLURAL NOUN

_____ with the crowd as we _____ awaited
PART OF THE BODY   ADVERB

the band's arrival. When they _____ walked onstage,
                              ADVERB

everyone cheered like wild _____. Then they began to
                           PLURAL NOUN

play their _____ music, and I sang along at the top of my
           ADJECTIVE

_____. When they finished and _____
PART OF THE BODY (PLURAL)   ADVERB

left the stage, I felt _____ because it was over. But then,
                      ADJECTIVE

to my _____ surprise, the crowd began yelling for more.
      ADJECTIVE

The band came back and played their hit song, " _____,
                                                ADJECTIVE

_____ Baby"! I was as happy as a/an _____.
SAME ADJECTIVE   NOUN

To make sure I'd remember this _____ experience for
                               ADJECTIVE

the rest of my _____, I bought myself a T-shirt with a
               NOUN

picture of the lead singer's _____ on it!
                            PART OF THE BODY

From ROCK 'N' ROLL MAD LIBS®. Copyright © 2010 by Price Stern Sloan,
a division of Penguin Young Readers Group, 345 Hudson Street, New York, NY 10014.

MAD LIBS® is fun to play with friends, but you can also play it by yourself! To begin with, DO NOT look at the story on the page below. Fill in the blanks on this page with the words called for. Then, using the words you have selected, fill in the blank spaces in the story.

Now you've created your own hilarious MAD LIBS® game!

CLASSICAL GENIUS

CELEBRITY _____

ADJECTIVE _____

NOUN _____

ADJECTIVE _____

PLURAL NOUN _____

LAST NAME _____

ADJECTIVE _____

PLURAL NOUN _____

PLURAL NOUN _____

ADJECTIVE _____

PLURAL NOUN _____

NOUN _____

PLURAL NOUN _____

ADJECTIVE _____

LETTER OF THE ALPHABET _____

MAD LIBS

CLASSICAL GENIUS

Are you familiar with the _____ Effect? It's a/an
CELEBRITY

_____ theory that says people should listen to classical
ADJECTIVE

music to become smarter than the average _____ . This
NOUN

hypothesis was first proposed by some _____ scientists
ADJECTIVE

who asked several _____ to listen to a few minutes
PLURAL NOUN

of music by musical greats such as Mozart, Bach, Beethoven,

and _____ . Then they gave their subjects a/an
LAST NAME

_____ test. The results showed that the _____
ADJECTIVE   PLURAL NOUN

who listened to the music scored better than the _____
PLURAL NOUN

who didn't. Apparently, the _____ theory is correct:
ADJECTIVE

Listening to classical music does help you memorize _____ ,
PLURAL NOUN

sharpen your _____ skills, and prevent _____ .
NOUN   PLURAL NOUN

So the next time you have a/an _____ test at school, just
ADJECTIVE

try listening to Beethoven before you take the exam—you're almost

guaranteed to get a/an _____ !
LETTER OF THE ALPHABET

MAD LIBS® is fun to play with friends, but you can also play it by yourself! To begin with, DO NOT look at the story on the page below. Fill in the blanks on this page with the words called for. Then, using the words you have selected, fill in the blank spaces in the story.

Now you've created your own hilarious MAD LIBS® game!

ON THE ROAD

PERSON IN ROOM _____

PLURAL NOUN _____

NOUN _____

A PLACE _____

A PLACE _____

ADJECTIVE _____

CELEBRITY _____

NOUN _____

NUMBER _____

PLURAL NOUN _____

ADJECTIVE _____

ADJECTIVE _____

PART OF THE BODY (PLURAL) _____

ANIMAL _____

NOUN _____

PART OF THE BODY _____

Dear Diary,

It's day thirty-two of my "Best of _____" World Tour. I've
\hspace{4cm} PERSON IN ROOM

been to so many cities and met so many _____ that I
\hspace{6cm} PLURAL NOUN

don't even remember where I am from one _____ to the
\hspace{6cm} NOUN

next. At tonight's concert in (the) _____, I accidentally
\hspace{5cm} A PLACE

shouted into the microphone, "Hello, (the) _____—how
\hspace{6cm} A PLACE

are you feelin' tonight?" Oops! Tonight I have to be sure to get a/an

_____ night's sleep because tomorrow I have an early TV
ADJECTIVE

interview with _____ on the _____ *Show*, then
\hspace{2cm} CELEBRITY \hspace{3cm} NOUN

I have to spend _____ hours signing _____ for
\hspace{2.5cm} NUMBER \hspace{4cm} PLURAL NOUN

_____ fans, and my afternoon is totally booked with seven
ADJECTIVE

_____ radio interviews. I'll keep my _____
ADJECTIVE \hspace{5.5cm} PART OF THE BODY (PLURAL)

crossed that I am able to take a quick _____-nap before
\hspace{5.5cm} ANIMAL

we perform our final _____ at the amphitheater
\hspace{3.5cm} NOUN

here in—wait, where are we again? I can hardly keep my

_____ on straight. Help!
PART OF THE BODY

MAD LIBS® is fun to play with friends, but you can also play it by yourself! To begin with, DO NOT look at the story on the page below. Fill in the blanks on this page with the words called for. Then, using the words you have selected, fill in the blank spaces in the story.

Now you've created your own hilarious MAD LIBS® game!

MAD LIBS MUSIC OFFER

VERB _____

ADJECTIVE _____

PLURAL NOUN_____

ADJECTIVE _____

PLURAL NOUN_____

VERB _____

PLURAL NOUN_____

ADJECTIVE _____

ADJECTIVE _____

VERB _____

ADJECTIVE _____

ADJECTIVE _____

ADJECTIVE _____

PLURAL NOUN_____

PERSON IN ROOM _____

NOUN _____

NUMBER _____

ADJECTIVE _____

PLURAL NOUN_____

MAD LIBS®

MAD LIBS MUSIC OFFER

They taught us how to love. They taught us how to _____.
<u>VERB</u>

And now they're back! This all-new collection of _____
<u>ADJECTIVE</u>

Ballads is guaranteed to knock your _____ off!
<u>PLURAL NOUN</u>

This _____ CD set contains twenty of the hottest
<u>ADJECTIVE</u>

mega-_____ of all time, including "Don't _____"
<u>PLURAL NOUN</u>   <u>VERB</u>

by _____ N' Roses, "_____ Enough" by
<u>PLURAL NOUN</u>   <u>ADJECTIVE</u>

_____ Yankees, and, for all you romantics out there,
<u>ADJECTIVE</u>

the unforgettable "To _____ with You" by Mr. _____,
<u>VERB</u>   <u>ADJECTIVE</u>

for when you're feeling _____ on a Saturday night. But
<u>ADJECTIVE</u>

wait—there's more! This _____ collection comes with a
<u>ADJECTIVE</u>

bonus DVD of music _____, featuring everything
<u>PLURAL NOUN</u>

_____ ever recorded! Yes, _____ fans, for
<u>PERSON IN ROOM</u>   <u>NOUN</u>

only _____ dollars and ninety-five cents, you can own
<u>NUMBER</u>

all of these _____ singles from yesteryear. Call now!
<u>ADJECTIVE</u>

This collection is not sold in _____!
<u>PLURAL NOUN</u>

From ROCK 'N' ROLL MAD LIBS®. Copyright © 2010 by Price Stern Sloan,
a division of Penguin Young Readers Group, 345 Hudson Street, New York, NY 10014.

MAD LIBS® is fun to play with friends, but you can also play it by yourself! To begin with, DO NOT look at the story on the page below. Fill in the blanks on this page with the words called for. Then, using the words you have selected, fill in the blank spaces in the story.

Now you've created your own hilarious MAD LIBS® game!

SING ALONG, PART 1

ADJECTIVE _____

PLURAL NOUN _____

NOUN _____

ADJECTIVE _____

ADJECTIVE _____

TYPE OF LIQUID _____

NOUN _____

NOUN _____

NOUN _____

NOUN _____

ANIMAL _____

ARTICLE OF CLOTHING _____

EXCLAMATION _____

NOUN _____

NOUN _____

NOUN _____

NOUN _____

MAD LIBS®

SING ALONG, PART 1

You may be a/an _____ musical expert now, but do you
ADJECTIVE

remember some of the first _____ you ever learned to
PLURAL NOUN

sing? Let's take a walk down _____ lane as we recall
NOUN

some _____ children's songs, Mad Libs style!
ADJECTIVE

1. The itsy-_____ spider went up the _____
   ADJECTIVE   TYPE OF LIQUID

   spout. Down came the rain and washed the _____
                                            NOUN

   out. Out came the _____ and dried up all the rain and
                     NOUN

   the itsy-bitsy spider went up the _____ again.
                                     NOUN

2. All around the mulberry _____, the _____ chased
                           NOUN   ANIMAL

   the weasel. The monkey stopped to pull up his _____.
                                                 ARTICLE OF CLOTHING

   "_____!" goes the weasel.
    EXCLAMATION

3. Rock-a-bye, _____, in the treetop. When the
               NOUN

   _____ blows, the cradle will rock. When the
   NOUN

   _____ breaks, the cradle will fall, and down will come
   NOUN

   baby, _____, and all.
         NOUN

MAD LIBS® is fun to play with friends, but you can also play it by yourself! To begin with, DO NOT look at the story on the page below. Fill in the blanks on this page with the words called for. Then, using the words you have selected, fill in the blank spaces in the story.

Now you've created your own hilarious MAD LIBS® game!

SING ALONG, PART 2

ADJECTIVE _____

NOUN _____

NOUN _____

VERB (PAST TENSE) _____

NOUN _____

NOUN _____

NOUN _____

TYPE OF FOOD _____

NOUN _____

ADJECTIVE _____

ADJECTIVE _____

PLURAL NOUN _____

NOUN _____

NOUN _____

ADJECTIVE _____

ADJECTIVE _____

MAD LIBS®

SING ALONG, PART 2

Now let's see how many of these _____ patriotic songs

ADJECTIVE

you know:

1. My _____ 'tis of thee, sweet _____ of

   NOUN   NOUN

   liberty, of thee I sing. Land where my fathers _____,

                                                   VERB (PAST TENSE)

   land of the pilgrims' pride, from every mountainside, let

   _____ ring!

   NOUN

2. Yankee-Doodle went to town, a-riding on a/an _____.

                                                  NOUN

   Stuck a feather in his _____ and called it _____.

                           NOUN   TYPE OF FOOD

   Yankee-Doodle, keep it up! Yankee-Doodle dandy. Mind the music

   and the _____, and with the girls be _____!

            NOUN   ADJECTIVE

3. And the rockets' _____ glare, the _____

                     ADJECTIVE   PLURAL NOUN

   bursting in air, gave proof through the night that our

   _____ was still there. Oh, say, does that star-spangled

   NOUN

   _____ yet wave, o'er the land of the _____

   NOUN   ADJECTIVE

   and the home of the _____.

                        ADJECTIVE

MAD LIBS® is fun to play with friends, but you can also play it by yourself! To begin with, DO NOT look at the story on the page below. Fill in the blanks on this page with the words called for. Then, using the words you have selected, fill in the blank spaces in the story.

Now you've created your own hilarious MAD LIBS® game!

FAN LETTER
TO A POP BAND

LAST NAME _____

CELEBRITY_____

NUMBER _____

ADJECTIVE _____

PLURAL NOUN_____

ADJECTIVE _____

NOUN _____

VERB ENDING IN "ING"_____

ADJECTIVE _____

A PLACE_____

ADJECTIVE _____

NOUN _____

PLURAL NOUN_____

PLURAL NOUN_____

ADVERB _____

ADJECTIVE _____

PERSON IN ROOM _____

MAD LIBS®
FAN LETTER
TO A POP BAND

Dear _____ Brothers,
       LAST NAME

I'm in the sixth grade at _____ Middle School, and I am
                       CELEBRITY

your number _____ fan. I have all of your _____
             NUMBER   ADJECTIVE

albums, but my favorite is *A Whole Lot of* _____. In my
                                    PLURAL NOUN

opinion, the best song you ever recorded is "_____
                                    ADJECTIVE

_____." Whenever it's on the radio, I can't stop
    NOUN

_____ to the beat! Now I have some _____
VERB ENDING IN "ING"   ADJECTIVE

questions for you. First, will you please come play a concert in my

hometown, (the) _____? Second, when will you be
               A PLACE

recording another _____ album? Finally, I read in
               ADJECTIVE

_____ *Beat* magazine that you guys like to eat fried
    NOUN

_____. I love them, too! I bet we have lots more in
PLURAL NOUN

common, and if we met, we'd be best _____ forever!
                                    PLURAL NOUN

Please write back _____!
                ADVERB

Your devoted and _____ fan,
               ADJECTIVE

_____
PERSON IN ROOM

MAD LIBS® is fun to play with friends, but you can also play it by yourself! To begin with, DO NOT look at the story on the page below. Fill in the blanks on this page with the words called for. Then, using the words you have selected, fill in the blank spaces in the story.

Now you've created your own hilarious MAD LIBS® game!

PROFILE OF THE BEATLES

ADJECTIVE _____

NOUN _____

A PLACE _____

NUMBER _____

NOUN _____

ADJECTIVE _____

NOUN _____

VERB _____

PERSON IN ROOM _____

PLURAL NOUN _____

NOUN _____

ADJECTIVE _____

VERB _____

NOUN _____

ADVERB _____

PLURAL NOUN _____

TYPE OF FOOD _____

NOUN _____

MAD LIBS

PROFILE OF THE BEATLES

The Beatles were not only the most _____ rock-and-roll
                                        ADJECTIVE

band of all time, they were probably the most critically acclaimed

_____ in the history of music. By 1985, this four-
        NOUN

member band from (the) _____ had sold over
                              A PLACE

_____ records internationally—more than any other
      NUMBER

_____ in history. Their _____ albums
      NOUN   ADJECTIVE

include *A Hard Day's* _____, *Let It* _____, and
                              NOUN   VERB

_____ *Road*. But the Beatles weren't just popular
   PERSON IN ROOM

because of their music. They were fashion _____ and
                                              PLURAL NOUN

_____ models for their _____ fans.
      NOUN   ADJECTIVE

Teenagers tried to dress like them, act like them, and _____
                                                            VERB

like them. "_____-mania" was a new phrase that referred
               NOUN

to the way teenage girls would cry _____, scream like
                                        ADVERB

_____, and faint at Beatles concerts. To sum it up, the
   PLURAL NOUN

Beatles were the biggest thing since sliced _____, and
                                                TYPE OF FOOD

no band before or since has been able to match their _____!
                                                          NOUN

From ROCK 'N' ROLL MAD LIBS®. Copyright © 2010 by Price Stern Sloan,
a division of Penguin Young Readers Group, 345 Hudson Street, New York, NY 10014.

MAD LIBS® is fun to play with friends, but you can also play it by yourself! To begin with, DO NOT look at the story on the page below. Fill in the blanks on this page with the words called for. Then, using the words you have selected, fill in the blank spaces in the story.

Now you've created your own hilarious MAD LIBS® game!

ACCEPTANCE SPEECH

EXCLAMATION _____

NOUN _____

NOUN _____

ADJECTIVE _____

NOUN _____

OCCUPATION _____

NOUN _____

ADJECTIVE _____

NOUN _____

OCCUPATION _____

PLURAL NOUN _____

VERB ENDING IN "ING" _____

ADJECTIVE _____

ADJECTIVE _____

NOUN _____

PART OF THE BODY _____

MAD LIBS®

ACCEPTANCE SPEECH

_____! I can't believe I won a/an _____
EXCLAMATION   NOUN

award! I have dreamed of this day since I was a little _____.
                                                          NOUN

I'd like to thank all of the _____ people who helped
                              ADJECTIVE

make this _____ become a reality, starting with my
            NOUN

_____ and, of course, my loving _____
OCCUPATION   NOUN

who supported me through thick and _____ . He
                                      ADJECTIVE

believed in my _____ when I was just a/an
                  NOUN

_____ in a small-town diner, struggling to make
OCCUPATION

_____ meet. He gave me the strength to keep on
PLURAL NOUN

_____ no matter what. To the other nominees, I
VERB ENDING IN "ING"

want to say how _____ I feel just to be nominated
                  ADJECTIVE

alongside you. Each one of you is a/an _____ artist. It's
                                        ADJECTIVE

been a long journey, but worth every _____! Thank
                                        NOUN

you from the bottom of my _____!
                            PART OF THE BODY

MAD LIBS® is fun to play with friends, but you can also play it by yourself! To begin with, DO NOT look at the story on the page below. Fill in the blanks on this page with the words called for. Then, using the words you have selected, fill in the blank spaces in the story.

Now you've created your own hilarious MAD LIBS® game!

THE JUDGES' DECISION

NOUN _____

NOUN _____

PART OF THE BODY _____

NOUN _____

ADVERB _____

PERSON IN ROOM (FEMALE) _____

ADJECTIVE _____

PLURAL NOUN_____

PERSON IN ROOM _____

ANIMAL _____

PLURAL NOUN _____

A PLACE _____

PERSON IN ROOM _____

ADJECTIVE _____

NOUN _____

NOUN _____

NOUN _____

ADJECTIVE _____

NOUN _____

MAD LIBS®
THE JUDGES' DECISION

When it was my turn to audition for _____ Idol, the reality
                                          NOUN

show where people compete to be the best solo _____,
                                                      NOUN

I sang from the depths of my very _____. When my
                                     PART OF THE BODY

song ended, I could hardly catch my _____ as
                                          NOUN

I _____ awaited the judges' response. First,
      ADVERB

_____ was very kind. She said, "Well the good
PERSON IN ROOM (FEMALE)

news is that you look _____, and you really connected
                           ADJECTIVE

with the _____ in that song." Then _____
            PLURAL NOUN   PERSON IN ROOM

said, "You know, _____, I dug your _____,"
                      ANIMAL   PLURAL NOUN

and I thought I really had a chance to make it to (the) _____!
                                                              A PLACE

But then mean, old _____ said, "Horrid. Terrible.
                        PERSON IN ROOM

_____. You sounded like an animal trapped inside a/an
  ADJECTIVE

_____." I gasped and shouted, "Well, you just don't
  NOUN

know anything about _____!" I stormed out of the
                          NOUN

_____. I was going to make it as a/an _____
  NOUN   ADJECTIVE

singer whether that judge from _____ Idol liked me or not!
                                     NOUN

From ROCK 'N' ROLL MAD LIBS®. Copyright © 2010 by Price Stern Sloan,
a division of Penguin Young Readers Group, 345 Hudson Street, New York, NY 10014.

MAD LIBS® is fun to play with friends, but you can also play it by yourself! To begin with, DO NOT look at the story on the page below. Fill in the blanks on this page with the words called for. Then, using the words you have selected, fill in the blank spaces in the story.

Now you've created your own hilarious MAD LIBS® game!

THE GOOD OL' DAYS

ADJECTIVE _____

PLURAL NOUN _____

ADJECTIVE _____

PLURAL NOUN _____

NOUN _____

NOUN _____

ADJECTIVE _____

PLURAL NOUN _____

PLURAL NOUN _____

PLURAL NOUN _____

ADJECTIVE _____

NOUN _____

PLURAL NOUN _____

ARTICLE OF CLOTHING (PLURAL) _____

ADJECTIVE _____

ADJECTIVE _____

EXCLAMATION _____

MAD LIBS®

THE GOOD OL' DAYS

Kids today! Who can figure out their _____ music? Back
                                          ADJECTIVE

in the good old _____, we didn't have _____
                   PLURAL NOUN   ADJECTIVE

mp3s and i-_____. We had a/an _____ and
              PLURAL NOUN   NOUN

a/an _____ and we'd bang them together to make drums.
        NOUN

We didn't have _____ guitars, so we'd use _____
                    ADJECTIVE   PLURAL NOUN

instead. We sang about love and _____. We didn't sing
                                     PLURAL NOUN

angry songs about _____. Our music had _____
                       PLURAL NOUN   ADJECTIVE

melodies, but the kids nowadays just smash a/an _____
                                                    NOUN

to bits onstage and call it music! They listen to groups like The

_____, who wear leather _____
   PLURAL NOUN   ARTICLE OF CLOTHING (PLURAL)

and _____ makeup. We used to listen to one
       ADJECTIVE

_____ guy with a banjo and, _____,
   ADJECTIVE   EXCLAMATION

we liked it!

From ROCK 'N' ROLL MAD LIBS®. Copyright © 2010 by Price Stern Sloan,
a division of Penguin Young Readers Group, 345 Hudson Street, New York, NY 10014.

MAD LIBS® is fun to play with friends, but you can also play it by yourself! To begin with, DO NOT look at the story on the page below. Fill in the blanks on this page with the words called for. Then, using the words you have selected, fill in the blank spaces in the story.

Now you've created your own hilarious MAD LIBS® game!

MUSIC HISTORY: MOZART

ADJECTIVE _____

PLURAL NOUN _____

ADJECTIVE _____

PLURAL NOUN _____

NOUN _____

PART OF THE BODY _____

ADVERB _____

NOUN _____

PLURAL NOUN _____

NOUN _____

ADJECTIVE _____

PLURAL NOUN _____

CELEBRITY _____

Wolfgang Amadeus Mozart was a/an _____ composer
ADJECTIVE

of the classical era. He created over six hundred musical

_____, many of which are still considered quite
PLURAL NOUN

_____. Mozart was what _____ today call a
ADJECTIVE   PLURAL NOUN

"child prodigy," which means he had talent far beyond that of the

average _____. For example, he could compose music
NOUN

inside his _____. He would imagine the piece and
PART OF THE BODY

then play it _____, without writing down a single
ADVERB

_____! Mozart gave concerts for kings, queens, and
NOUN

wealthy _____ who rejoiced in his astonishing
PLURAL NOUN

_____. This _____ genius influenced many
NOUN   ADJECTIVE

future _____, including Ludwig van Beethoven and
PLURAL NOUN

_____!
CELEBRITY

MAD LIBS® is fun to play with friends, but you can also play it by yourself! To begin with, DO NOT look at the story on the page below. Fill in the blanks on this page with the words called for. Then, using the words you have selected, fill in the blank spaces in the story.

Now you've created your own hilarious MAD LIBS® game!

ALL ABOUT MUSIC

PLURAL NOUN _____

ADJECTIVE _____

ADJECTIVE _____

NOUN _____

NOUN _____

ADJECTIVE _____

NOUN _____

NOUN _____

NOUN _____

COLOR _____

PLURAL NOUN _____

NOUN _____

ADJECTIVE _____

PLURAL NOUN _____

MAD LIBS®

ALL ABOUT MUSIC

There are almost as many types of music as there are _____
                                                    PLURAL NOUN

in the world. Here is a quick guide to some of today's most

_____ types of music and how they are interpreted:
ADJECTIVE

1) **Love songs** tend to be slow and _____, allowing the
                                          ADJECTIVE

   singer to tell his love, "You are the _____ of my life" or
                                              NOUN

   "I want to hold your _____."
                            NOUN

2) **Country music** usually tells a/an _____ story.
                                              ADJECTIVE

   Sometimes the song is about a/an _____ who loses his
                                          NOUN

   job, his wife, and even his _____ all at once.
                                    NOUN

3) **The blues** is all about _____ and suffering, and it gets
                                    NOUN

   its name from the expression, "feeling _____." Artists
                                              COLOR

   express their inner _____ through the blues.
                          PLURAL NOUN

4) **Rock 'n' roll**'s roots lay mainly in blues, country, gospel, jazz, and

   _____. It is performed with _____ energy and
        NOUN   ADJECTIVE

   has influenced lifestyles and fashion as well as attitudes and

   _____.
     PLURAL NOUN

From ROCK 'N' ROLL MAD LIBS®. Copyright © 2010 by Price Stern Sloan,
a division of Penguin Young Readers Group, 345 Hudson Street, New York, NY 10014.

MAD LIBS® is fun to play with friends, but you can also play it by yourself! To begin with, DO NOT look at the story on the page below. Fill in the blanks on this page with the words called for. Then, using the words you have selected, fill in the blank spaces in the story.

Now you've created your own hilarious MAD LIBS® game!

STORY OF A ONE-HIT WONDER

PLURAL NOUN _____

NOUN _____

ADJECTIVE _____

PART OF THE BODY _____

ADJECTIVE _____

ADJECTIVE _____

NOUN _____

ADJECTIVE _____

LAST NAME _____

PLURAL NOUN _____

ADVERB _____

PART OF THE BODY _____

ADJECTIVE _____

NOUN _____

PLURAL NOUN _____

ADJECTIVE _____

A PLACE _____

MAD LIBS®
STORY OF A
ONE-HIT WONDER

The Mighty _____ were a one-_____ wonder,
            PLURAL NOUN   NOUN

famous for their _____ song, "In Your _____."
             ADJECTIVE   PART OF THE BODY

Where is this _____ band today? After hitting it big, they
           ADJECTIVE

started to have _____ creative differences. They went
           ADJECTIVE

from superstardom to a/an _____-shattering breakup.
                  NOUN

The lead singer, known for his _____ personality, wanted
                    ADJECTIVE

to change the band's name to _____'s _____.
                    LAST NAME   PLURAL NOUN

The rest of the band _____ refused. No one could see eye
               ADVERB

to _____, and the bassist decided to leave the
   PART OF THE BODY

_____ band and pursue his lifelong dream of professional
  ADJECTIVE

_____-weaving. The drummer left to teach music to high
  NOUN

school _____. The lead singer was the only one left. But
      PLURAL NOUN

don't feel too bad—he has now become a/an _____
                             ADJECTIVE

Internet sensation with a video of himself playing "Sweet Home,

(the) _____" on the kazoo!
   A PLACE

MAD LIBS® is fun to play with friends, but you can also play it by yourself! To begin with, DO NOT look at the story on the page below. Fill in the blanks on this page with the words called for. Then, using the words you have selected, fill in the blank spaces in the story.

Now you've created your own hilarious MAD LIBS® game!

GUESS WHO?

A PLACE _____

NUMBER _____

OCCUPATION _____

NOUN _____

ADJECTIVE _____

PLURAL NOUN_____

PLURAL NOUN_____

PLURAL NOUN_____

NOUN _____

NOUN _____

PLURAL NOUN_____

ADJECTIVE _____

ADJECTIVE _____

MAD LIBS®
GUESS WHO?

She was born in (the) _____ , Michigan, in 1942 and
                    A PLACE

started recording songs when she was only _____ years
                                          NUMBER

old. Her nickname is "The _____ of Soul" and she was the
                          OCCUPATION

first woman to be inducted into the Rock and Roll _____
                                                   NOUN

of Fame. She has lent her _____ voice to many public
                          ADJECTIVE

events, including the inaugurations of two American _____ .
                                                     PLURAL NOUN

The National Academy of Recording Arts and _____ has
                                            PLURAL NOUN

awarded her seventeen Grammy _____ , including the
                              PLURAL NOUN

prestigious "Living _____ Award" in 1991. One of her
                     NOUN

greatest hits was called "I Never Loved a/an _____ the Way
                                              NOUN

I Loved You," but she is best known for her megasmash, "Chain of

_____ ." Just who is this _____ diva? Of course,
 PLURAL NOUN   ADJECTIVE

it's the truly _____ Aretha Franklin!
               ADJECTIVE

MAD LIBS® is fun to play with friends, but you can also play it by yourself! To begin with, DO NOT look at the story on the page below. Fill in the blanks on this page with the words called for. Then, using the words you have selected, fill in the blank spaces in the story.

Now you've created your own hilarious MAD LIBS® game!

ROCK STAR COMMERCIAL

ADJECTIVE _____

ADJECTIVE _____

NOUN _____

ADJECTIVE _____

NUMBER _____

ADJECTIVE _____

ADJECTIVE _____

PLURAL NOUN _____

NOUN _____

NOUN _____

NOUN _____

ADJECTIVE _____

PLURAL NOUN _____

PART OF THE BODY _____

NOUN _____

PLURAL NOUN _____

ADJECTIVE _____

ADJECTIVE _____

ADVERB _____

SAME ADVERB _____

ADJECTIVE _____

NOUN _____

MAD LIBS®

ROCK STAR COMMERCIAL

This is a/an _____ *rock star TV Commercial to be*
                ADJECTIVE

performed by a/an _____ *person in the room:*
                    ADJECTIVE

When I'm on tour with my _____, I have to be
                              NOUN

_____. That's why I drink at least _____ Rock 'n'
ADJECTIVE   NUMBER

Roll Energy Sodas a day. But it's not just for _____ rockers
                                                  ADJECTIVE

like me, it's a/an _____ pick-me-up for _____
                      ADJECTIVE   PLURAL NOUN

from all walks of life: the stressed-out _____ driver, the
                                            NOUN

overworked computer _____, or the exhausted high-
                        NOUN

fashion _____. It's a/an _____ beverage with a
           NOUN   ADJECTIVE

special combination of natural _____ that vitalizes the
                                  PLURAL NOUN

mind and _____. I drink one whenever I record a new
          PART OF THE BODY

_____ or autograph _____ for my fans. I even
     NOUN   PLURAL NOUN

have one in the middle of a/an _____ concert to give my
                                  ADJECTIVE

_____ singing a boost! People who need to perform
ADJECTIVE

_____ should drink _____. So try my favorite
   ADVERB   SAME ADVERB

_____ beverage and jump-start your _____ today!
ADJECTIVE   NOUN

From ROCK 'N' ROLL MAD LIBS®. Copyright © 2010 by Price Stern Sloan,
a division of Penguin Young Readers Group, 345 Hudson Street, New York, NY 10014.

MAD LIBS® is fun to play with friends, but you can also play it by yourself! To begin with, DO NOT look at the story on the page below. Fill in the blanks on this page with the words called for. Then, using the words you have selected, fill in the blank spaces in the story.

Now you've created your own hilarious MAD LIBS® game!

PROM REVIEW

ADJECTIVE _____

PERSON IN ROOM _____

ADJECTIVE _____

PLURAL NOUN _____

ADJECTIVE _____

NOUN _____

PLURAL NOUN _____

ADJECTIVE _____

PLURAL NOUN _____

ADJECTIVE _____

NOUN _____

PERSON IN ROOM (MALE) _____

PERSON IN ROOM (FEMALE) _____

OCCUPATION _____

NUMBER _____

PLURAL NOUN _____

NOUN _____

NOUN _____

MAD LIBS®

PROM REVIEW

Here's a/an _____ review of the senior prom written by
　　　　　　　ADJECTIVE

_____ for our _____ high school paper:
PERSON IN ROOM　　　　　　ADJECTIVE

The prom last night was more fun than a barrel of _____!
　　　　　　　　　　　　　　　　　　　　　　　PLURAL NOUN

The _____ design committee decorated the gym in an
　　　ADJECTIVE

"Under the _____" theme, with shimmery blue streamers
　　　　　　NOUN

and inflated _____ everywhere. It looked absolutely
　　　　　　　PLURAL NOUN

_____. When the band, the Dirty _____,
ADJECTIVE　　　　　　　　　　　　　　　　　PLURAL NOUN

took to the stage, they played lots of _____
　　　　　　　　　　　　　　　　　　　　ADJECTIVE

songs including their hit single, "I Wanna Rock with a/an

_____." During a break in the music, _____
NOUN　　　　　　　　　　　　　　　　　PERSON IN ROOM (MALE)

and _____ were elected Prom King and
　PERSON IN ROOM (FEMALE)

_____, and an elegant _____-course dinner
OCCUPATION　　　　　　　　　　　NUMBER

was served. It included a choice of filet mignon, roasted

_____, or poached _____. When all was said
PLURAL NOUN　　　　　　　NOUN

and done, it was truly a/an _____ to remember.
　　　　　　　　　　　　　NOUN

MAD LIBS® is fun to play with friends, but you can also play it by yourself! To begin with, DO NOT look at the story on the page below. Fill in the blanks on this page with the words called for. Then, using the words you have selected, fill in the blank spaces in the story.

Now you've created your own hilarious MAD LIBS® game!

BAND FAN
CLUB MEETING

ADJECTIVE _____

PLURAL NOUN _____

PART OF THE BODY _____

PERSON IN ROOM _____

ADJECTIVE _____

NOUN _____

PERSON IN ROOM _____

ARTICLE OF CLOTHING (PLURAL) _____

PART OF THE BODY (PLURAL) _____

ADJECTIVE _____

ADJECTIVE _____

NUMBER _____

ADJECTIVE _____

ADJECTIVE _____

NOUN _____

EXCLAMATION _____

MAD LIBS®
BAND FAN
CLUB MEETING

Hear ye, hear ye! This meeting of the _____ _____

ADJECTIVE   PLURAL NOUN

fan club is called to order. First, I would like to give a/an

_____-felt thanks to _____ for baking this

PART OF THE BODY   PERSON IN ROOM

_____ cake in the shape of the band's _____.

ADJECTIVE   NOUN

Next, I'm happy to announce that _____ has arrived with

PERSON IN ROOM

what we have all been waiting for: _____ with

ARTICLE OF CLOTHING (PLURAL)

pictures of the band's _____ on them! I'm sure we

PART OF THE BODY (PLURAL)

will all wear them with _____ pride. Finally, I would like

ADJECTIVE

to form a new _____ committee to oversee the fan letter

ADJECTIVE

project. I'm hoping that if we can send at least _____

NUMBER

_____ letters to the band, they will consider doing a

ADJECTIVE

concert in our _____ town—or at least send us

ADJECTIVE

an autographed _____. All those in favor, say,

NOUN

" _____ !"

EXCLAMATION

This book is published by

PSS!
PRICE STERN SLOAN

whose other splendid titles include
such literary classics as

Best of Mad Libs®	Mad Libs® Collector's Edition
Camp Daze Mad Libs®	Mad Libs® for President
Christmas Carol Mad Libs®: Very Merry Songs & Stories	Mad Libs® from Outer Space
	Mad Libs® in Love
Christmas Fun Mad Libs®	Mad Libs® on the Road
Cool Mad Libs®	Mad Mad Mad Mad Mad Libs®
Dear Valentine Letters Mad Libs®	Monster Mad Libs®
Dinosaur Mad Libs®	Night of the Living Mad Libs®
Diva Girl Mad Libs®	Off-the-Wall Mad Libs®
Family Tree Mad Libs®	Peace, Love, and Mad Libs®
Goofy Mad Libs®	Pirates Mad Libs®
Grab Bag Mad Libs®	Prime-Time Mad Libs®
Graduation Mad Libs®	Slam Dunk Mad Libs®
Grand Slam Mad Libs®	Sleepover Party Mad Libs®
Happy Birthday Mad Libs®	Son of Mad Libs®
Haunted Mad Libs®	Sooper Dooper Mad Libs®
Holly, Jolly Mad Libs®	Spooky Mad Libs®
Kid Libs Mad Libs®	Straight "A" Mad Libs®
Letters From Camp Mad Libs®	The Original #1 Mad Libs®
Letters to Mom & Dad Mad Libs®	Upside Down Mad Libs®
	Vacation Fun Mad Libs®
Mad About Animals Mad Libs®	Winter Games Mad Libs®
Mad Libs® 40th Anniversary	You've Got Mad Libs®

and many, many more!
Mad Libs® are available wherever books are sold.